The MAILBOX®

Social Skills
for Little Learners

Fun activities for learning positive behaviors

- Listening
- Manners
- Persevering
- Being Safe
- Teamwork

- Self-Control
- Cooperating
- Being Brave
- Sharing
- Getting Along

Managing Editors: Kimberly Brugger-Murphy and Brenda Miner

Editorial Team: Becky S. Andrews, Randi Austin, Diane Badden, Pamela Ballingall, Janet Boyce, Tricia Brown, Kimberley Bruck, Karen A. Brudnak, Marie E. Cecchini, Pam Crane, Denise Crook, Roxanne LaBell Dearman, Beth Deki, Lynette Dickerson, Sarah Foreman, Deborah Garmon, Deborah Gibbone, Paula Glass, Tazmen Hansen, Marsha Heim, Lori Z. Henry, Jennie Jensen, Debra Liverman, Kitty Lowrance, Dorothy C. McKinney, Thad H. McLaurin, Sharon Murphy, Jennifer Nunn, Keely Peasner, Tina Petersen, Mark Rainey, Greg D. Rieves, Hope Rodgers, Donna K. Teal, Rachael Traylor, Carole Watkins

Features favorite story characters!

www.themailbox.com

©2009 The Mailbox® Books
All rights reserved.
ISBN10 #1-56234-898-1 • ISBN13 #978-1-56234-898-4

Printed in the United States
10 9 8 7 6 5 4 3 2 1

Table of Contents

Social Skills for Little Learners • ©The Mailbox® Books • TEC61241

What's Inside

50 fun teaching activities

10 pull-out mini posters

over **35** pages of
timesaving reproducibles

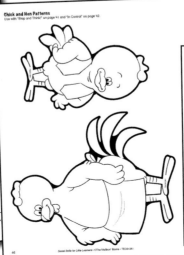

Using the Mini Posters

Try these suggestions!

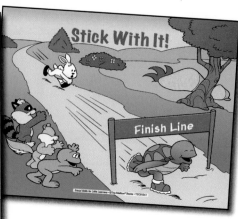

Full-color mini poster

- Use a mini poster to help youngsters recall the challenges faced by the story character(s) and describe the learning that takes place.

- Post the mini posters near your group-time area. Refer to the posters when praising student behaviors and when reminding little ones of positive behaviors.

- Place each mini poster in a clear plastic page protector. Lay a collection of posters facedown in your group-time area. Randomly turn over one poster at a time and invite students to share ways they practice each behavior.

- Tape a laminated mini poster on chart paper. Then write on the paper in each child's own words ways he practices the behavior at school or home.

Black-and-white mini poster

- Send each child home with a copy of a mini poster (or attach a copy to your class newsletter). Ask that each family talk about the poster and display it in their home to remind everyone of this positive behavior.

- Invite a child to color a copy of the mini poster and take it home to share with his family.

- Copy a poster four times at 50 percent reduction and then use the reduced artwork to make a master copy like the one shown. Use the master copy to make several sheets of quarter-page notes. When a youngster is observed practicing the positive behavior, write a brief explanation on the back of a note and send it home with the child.

Use Listening Ears

Little ones will be all ears when listening to Peter Rabbit's adventure in *The Tale of Peter Rabbit* by Beatrix Potter. No doubt youngsters will notice that Peter has difficulty listening!

Mother Says

With this variation of Simon Says, your little bunnies practice listening skills. Give each student two bunny ear cutouts (see page 10) and a paper strip and help her make a headband similar to the one shown. Have students don their headbands. Tell them you are Mrs. Rabbit and they are your baby bunnies. Then give them a direction, such as "hop five times." Play additional rounds as time allows.

Where's Peter?

Encourage youngsters to use their listening skills with this fun activity. In advance, hide a stuffed rabbit (Peter) in the school. Then post clues about Peter's whereabouts throughout the school. Tell youngsters that Peter is hiding and his mother needs them to help find him. Encourage students to listen carefully as you read the first clue, and then have youngsters determine where they need to go. Continue leading students through the clues until Peter is found, praising students' listening skills throughout the game.

Mr. McGregor's Garden

Little ones help Peter find great hiding places in Mr. McGregor's garden. Give each student a Peter Rabbit cutout (see page 10) and a copy of Mr. McGregor's garden on page 11. Tell students it is very important that they listen carefully to your directions so Mr. McGregor does not find Peter. Use a positional word and location, such as beside the watering can, to name a hiding place for Peter. Then instruct each student to put Peter in the corresponding location on his map. Repeat the activity using different positional words.

Colorful Bunny

Students listen carefully to color these cute bunnies. Give each student a copy of the bunny reproducible on page 12. Say, "Color the inside of the bunny's ears pink." Then watch carefully to make sure youngsters listened to the direction. Continue giving students directions to add other details, such as the ones shown.

Detail Suggestions
Color your bunny's nose pink.
Draw whiskers on your bunny.
Color brown spots on your bunny.
Draw grass under your bunny.
Draw a carrot in the grass for your bunny to eat.

"Berry" Good Parfaits

Little ones use their listening skills to make a "berry" good snack! Instruct each child to put a scoop of blueberries in a cup. Then have him put a scoop of whipped topping over the blueberries. Repeat the process with strawberries and another layer of whipped topping. Finally, tell him to sprinkle graham cracker crumbs on top before he eats his yummy treat.

Be a Good Listener

Be a Good Listener

Bunny Ear Patterns

Use with "Mother Says" on page 5.

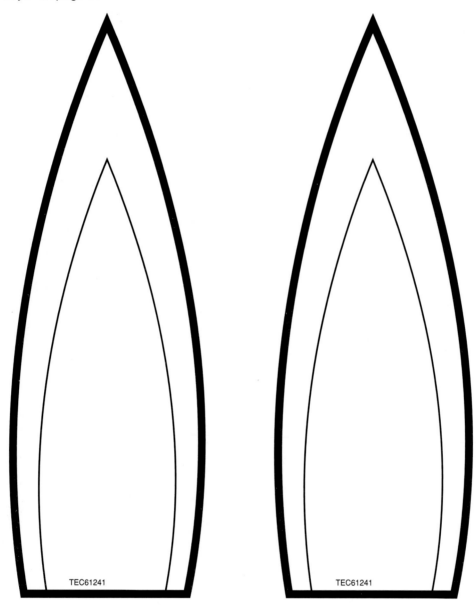

TEC61241

TEC61241

Peter Rabbit Patterns

Use with "Mr. McGregor's Garden" on page 6.

TEC61241

TEC61241

TEC61241

TEC61241

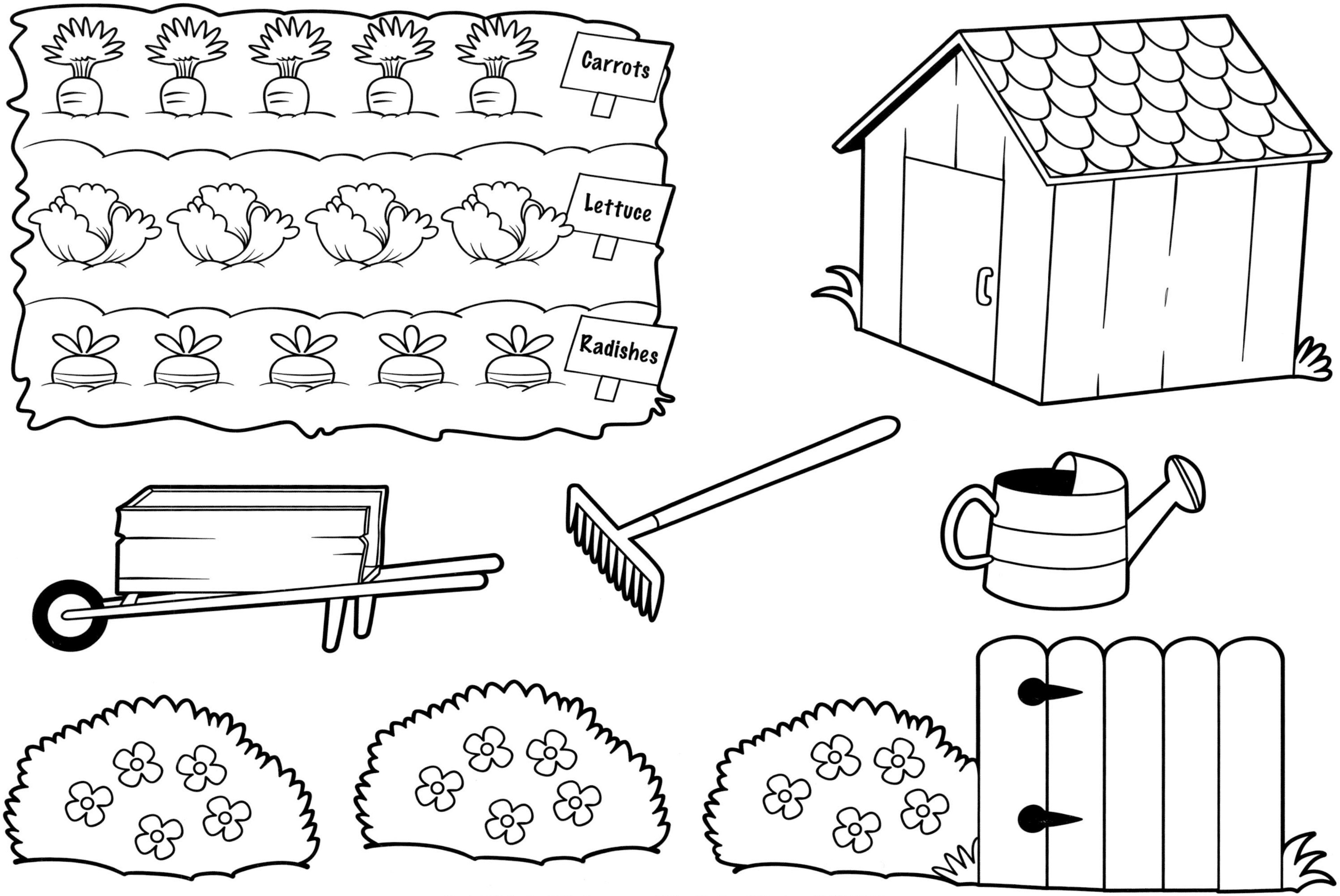
Carrots
Lettuce
Radishes

Note to the teacher: Use with “Mr. McGregor’s Garden” on page 6.

Note to the teacher: Use with "Colorful Bunny" on page 6.

Mind Your Manners

Read aloud a favorite version of *Goldilocks and the Three Bears* to prepare students for these fun ideas. Your little ones will be more than happy to assist Goldilocks in becoming a polite guest.

I'm Sorry

Goldilocks accidentally breaks Baby Bear's chair and she never apologizes. Ask little ones what they should do if they break something that belongs to another person, leading them to conclude that they should apologize. Have youngsters pretend to be Goldilocks. Then invite them to dictate a note of apology to Baby Bear as you write their words on a sheet of chart paper.

Dear Baby Bear,
  I am very sorry I broke your chair. It was an accident. I would like to help you fix it.

Sincerely,

Goldilocks

Teaching Goldilocks

With this song, youngsters teach Goldilocks to be a guest who is always welcome.

(sung to the tune of "This Old Man")

Goldilocks, don't be rude.
Don't eat someone else's food!
When you use good manners,
Things will turn out fine.
Wait until you're asked to dine.

Goldilocks, show some care.
Do not break another's chair!
When you use good manners,
There will be no mistake.
Nothing in the house will break.

May I?

With this role-playing activity, little ones pretend that Goldilocks uses her best manners. Prepare a set of stick puppets using a copy of the character patterns on page 18. Give one student the Goldilocks puppet and a classmate one of the bear puppets. Instruct Goldilocks to politely ask the bear if she may do a desired activity. For example, she might say, "Mother Bear, may I sit in your chair?" Then have the bear respond, "Yes, you may." Continue until each student has had a turn.

Nice or Not

Have each child color and cut out a copy of the bear faces on page 19 and glue them to opposite sides of a paper plate. Describe a realistic situation, such as "Nate walked into a friend's house without being invited." Instruct each student to hold his plate to show the face that corresponds with the manners described. Continue the activity using different situations.

Terrific Table Manners

Encourage polite table manners with this simple idea. Place on a plastic plate a class supply of miniature rice cakes and then give each student a napkin. Carry the tray to a student and ask, "Would you like a rice cake?" Prompt him to say either "Yes, please" or "No, thank you." Then serve the youngster a rice cake if he desires one. Encourage him to wait until everyone has been served before he begins to eat.

For a related reproducible student activity, go to page 20.

Manners Are Important

Manners Are Important

Character Patterns

Use with "May I?" on page 14.

TEC61241

TEC61241

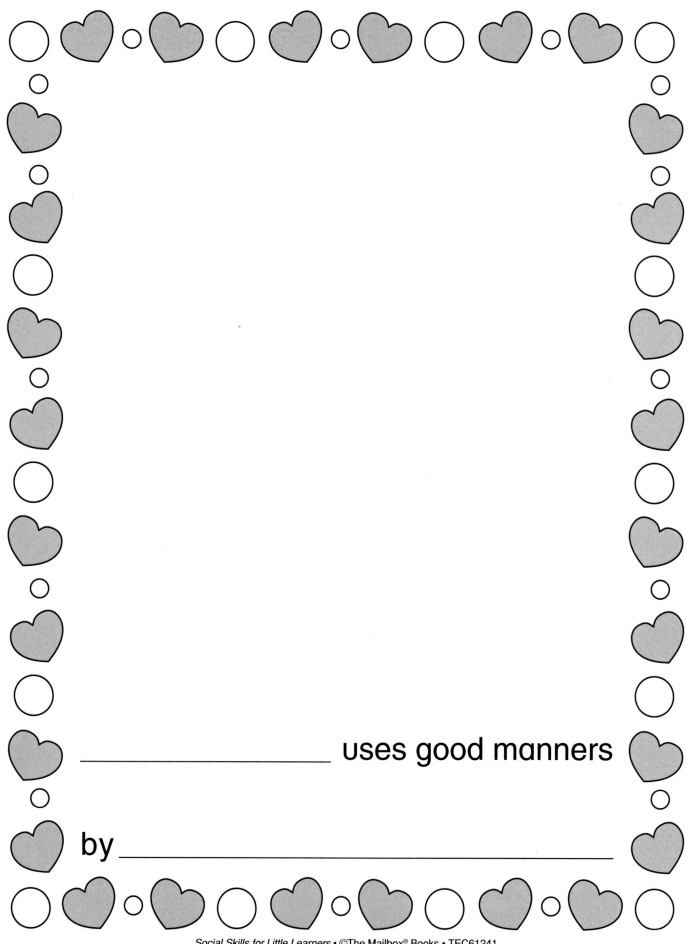

_____ uses good manners

by _____

Note to the teacher: On a copy of this page, have a child draw herself using good manners. Then help her write her name and complete the sentence. Bind youngsters' pages together to make a class book titled "We Have Good Manners."

Finish Line

Stick With It!

Read aloud your favorite version of *The Tortoise and the Hare* to show youngsters that hard work and determination pay off in the end. Then invite students to join in this fun-filled collection of activities about the social skill of perseverance.

Practice Pays Off

Lead a discussion that emphasizes how Tortoise pursued his goal and did not give up. Next, have each youngster name a school-related skill, such as cutting with scissors or writing his name, he will need to practice to accomplish. Write his response on a sheet of paper. Then have him draw and color a picture to match his words. Keep the paper handy; then adorn it with turtle stickers to reward him for his persistence when he accomplishes the task!

I am learning to zip my coat.

(sung to the tune of "The Wheels on the Bus")

Fast tempo:
The hare in the race moved oh so fast, oh so fast, oh so fast.
The hare in the race moved oh so fast but didn't stay on task!

Slow tempo:
The tortoise in the race moved oh so slow, oh so slow, oh so slow.
The tortoise in the race moved oh so slow but never gave up!

He crawled till he reached the finish line, finish line, finish line.
He crawled till he reached the finish line and then he won the race!

Stay on Task

With this activity, youngsters are reminded that Hare could have won the race if he had stayed on task! Have one child (Hare) stand at a masking tape starting line. Have a second child (Tortoise) kneel at the line. Have Hare hop toward a finish line as you lead the group in singing the first verse of the song shown. When the verse ends, Hare lies down and pretends to take a nap. Then Tortoise crawls toward the finish line as you lead the group in singing the remaining verses. When the song ends, Hare "wakes up" and sees Tortoise win the race!

An Amazing Finish

With this activity, students learn that they can accomplish tricky tasks if they just keep trying! Draw a maze, similar to the one shown, on poster board and place a toy turtle at Start. Invite a youngster to move the turtle along the maze, trying to find the path that leads to Finish. If he reaches a dead end, instruct him to turn the turtle around and look for a new path. Encourage him to continue until he finds the path that leads the turtle to Finish. Be sure to give lots of praise for his determination and perseverance!

The Big Race

With this catchy tune, youngsters are reminded of how determination and persistence helped Tortoise win the race!

(sung to the tune of "The Hokey-Pokey")

The tortoise and the hare
Ran a big race one day.
The tortoise won the race
But took his time along the way.
He moved so slow and steady,
But he kept his pace up too.
That's what helped him get through!

We Know Our Colors!

A Classroom Full of Winners

Color and cut out an enlarged copy of the tortoise pattern from page 26. Then attach the tortoise to a wall decorated with a finish line, as shown. Choose a skill youngsters have just started to work on, such as identifying shapes or colors, and title the display accordingly. As each student succeeds in the skill, write his name on a ribbon cutout and attach the cutout to the board.

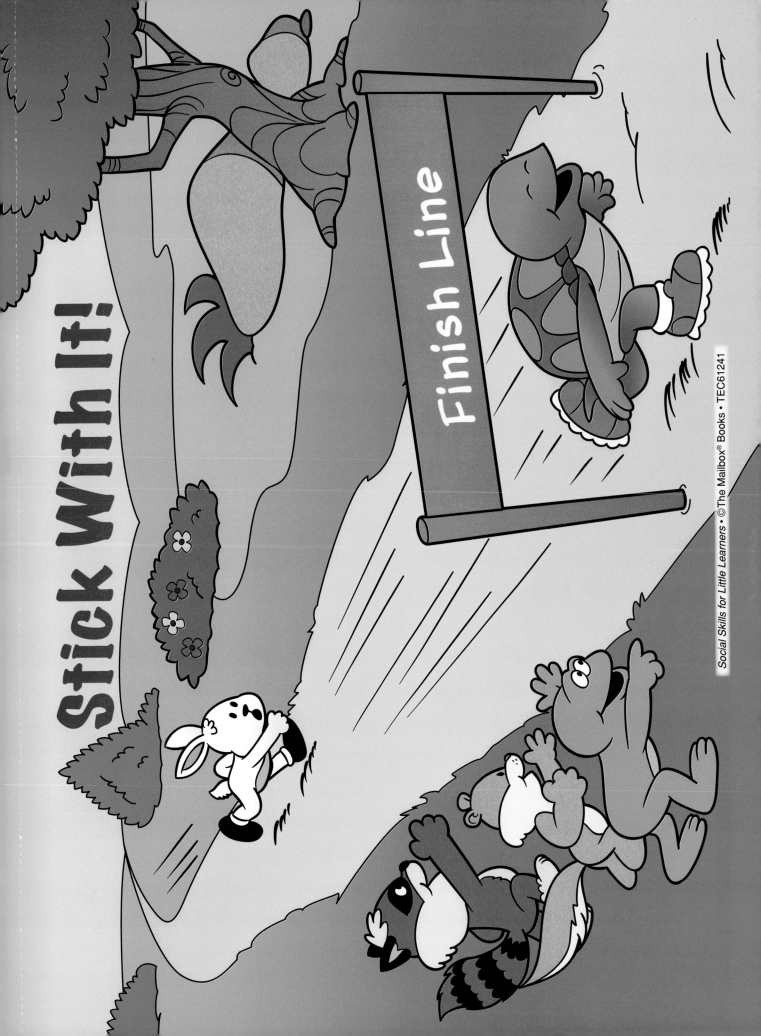

Stick With It!

Finish Line

Tortoise Pattern
Use with "A Classroom Full of Winners" on page 22.

TEC61241

Staying Safe

Read aloud a favorite version of *Little Red Riding Hood* to get little ones ready for these fun activities. Youngsters will agree that the little girl, along with her mother and grandmother, need some safety lessons!

Warning Flags

During the story, Little Red Riding Hood does many things that are not very safe. Use red copies of the flag patterns from page 32 and craft sticks to make a flag for each child. Tell students that their flags are red because it is a color that is often used to represent danger. Read aloud *Little Red Riding Hood* and have youngsters raise their flags each time Little Red Riding Hood does something that is unsafe. Each time students raise their flags, invite them to discuss their reasoning.

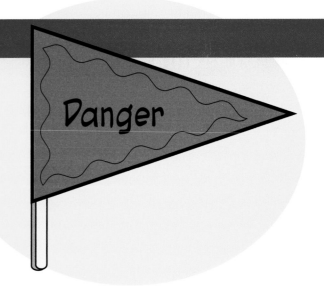

Danger

Walk Away

Where are you going, Little Red Riding Hood?

Little Red Riding Hood's problems begin when she stops to talk to the wolf. This activity teaches little ones a simple way to avoid making the same mistake. Use the patterns on page 33 to make stick puppets. Have two students use the puppets to reenact Little Red Riding Hood being approached by the wolf. Instruct the wolf to talk to Little Red Riding Hood, but direct Little Red Riding Hood to simply walk away from the wolf. Continue until each student gets a chance to play a character.

I pledge to stay safe by...

...not talking to strangers.

...staying close to my parents.

...not talking to wolves.

...not opening the door to strangers.

...listening to my parents.

Safety Pledge

Little ones demonstrate an understanding of personal safety rules with this activity. Post a sheet of poster board labeled with "I pledge to stay safe by..." Ask little ones to name ways they can keep themselves safe, such as by not talking to strangers or not wandering away from their parents. Write students' ideas on the poster. When students are finished naming ways to stay safe, invite each youngster to sign the poster. Display the completed pledge in your classroom.

Grandma's Blunder

When the wolf knocks on Grandma's door, she tells him to come in without first checking to see who is there. Have a pair of students stand on opposite sides of a closed door. Instruct the student outside to knock on the door. Direct the student inside to ask, "Who is it?" and listen for a reply. Then have the child on the inside ask you for permission before opening the door. Continue until each student has had a turn being on each side of the door.

Sorting Strangers

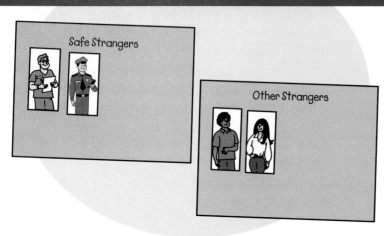

Help youngsters understand that some strangers are safe to talk to. Color and cut apart a copy of the picture cards from page 34 and place them in a small bag. Post two sheets of construction paper labeled as shown and set the bag and a glue stick nearby. Invite a volunteer to take a card from the bag and show it to her classmates. Encourage little ones to discuss if it's all right to talk to the stranger shown and then have the volunteer glue the card on the corresponding sheet of paper. Continue as described for each remaining card.

Never Talk to Strangers

Never Talk to Strangers

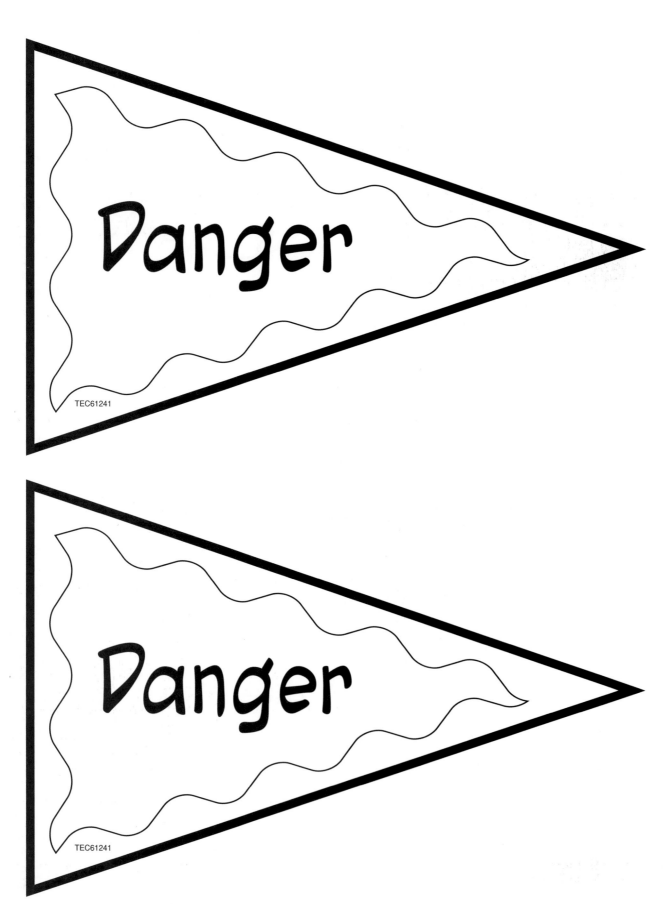

TEC61241

TEC61241

Social Skills for Little Learners • ©The Mailbox® Books • TEC61241

Picture Cards

Use with "Sorting Strangers" on page 28.

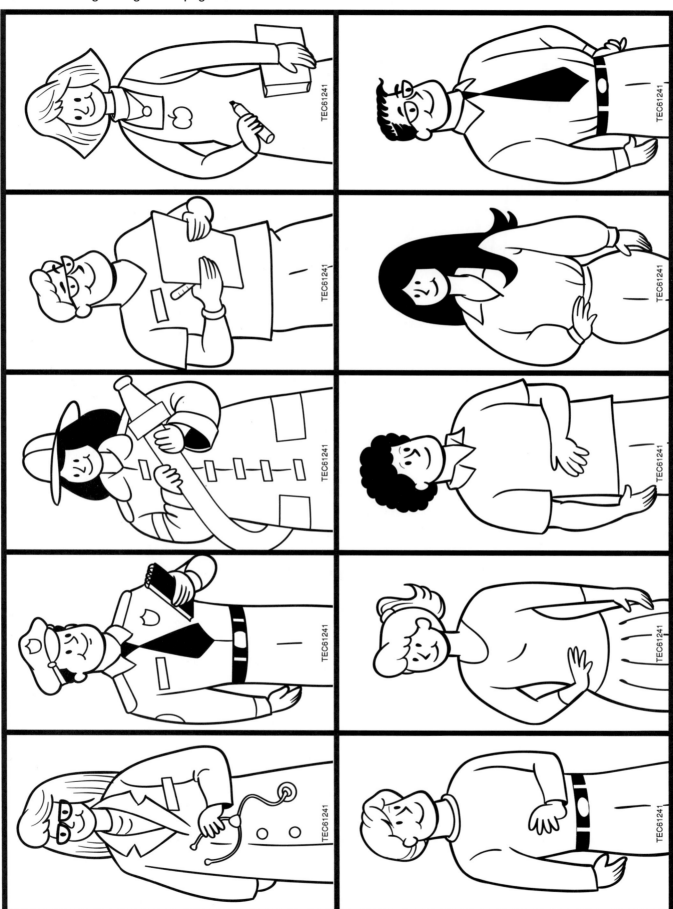

Social Skills for Little Learners • ©The Mailbox® Books • TEC61241

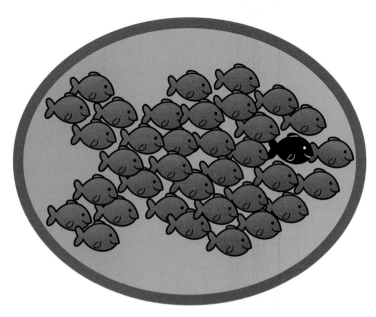

We're a Team!

Read aloud *Swimmy* by Leo Lionni to help your little ones learn how teamwork gets a job done. Then invite youngsters to participate in these engaging activities that highlight the benefits of teamwork.

One Big Fish!

To outsmart a hungry tuna, Swimmy and the red fish swim close together so they look like the biggest fish in the sea! Inspire youngsters to work together to create their own big red fish. Draw a large fish outline on light blue bulletin board paper. Have students work together to fill in the outline with red fingerprints (fish). Draw a little black fish for the eye. Then have youngsters decorate the paper around the fish. Display the project and give students a big thumbs-up for a fantastic group effort!

Go Away, Tuna!

With this game, youngsters work together to unite red fish so they can scare away a lurking tuna. To prepare, place a plastic hoop in an open area with an oversize tuna cutout nearby. Divide the class into several teams. Then give each student a red fish cutout (see page 40). On your signal, a child from each team runs to the hoop, places his fish inside, and then runs back to his team where he tags a teammate to place his fish in the hoop. Encourage the remaining youngsters to enthusiastically cheer on their classmates! Continue the game until all the fish are together in the hoop, and then whisk the tuna away with great fanfare!

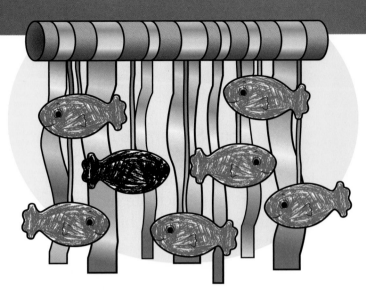

Under the Sea

Students highlight how well they work as a group when they make this class mobile! To begin, have students cut out white copies of the fish patterns on page 40. Have them color the fish red. Then help youngsters use yarn to suspend their fish from a cardboard tube. Also suspend blue cellophane strips and a black fish cutout from the tube. Then hang the mobile as a proud display of class teamwork!

Hooray, Teamwork!

Lead youngsters in singing this fun song to help celebrate the remarkable teamwork displayed by Swimmy and the little red fish!

(sung to the tune of "The Itsy-Bitsy Spider")

Swimmy and some red fish
Swam along one day.
A tuna ate the red fish,
But Swimmy got away!
Then Swimmy showed his new friends
The teamwork they should do.
They could all work together
And scare that tuna too!

Beat the Clock!

With this activity, little ones are sure to learn the value of teamwork as they race against time! To begin, scatter blocks on the floor and place an empty box nearby. Time a volunteer to see how long it takes him to pick up the blocks and place them in the box. Then write down his time and applaud his efforts. Scatter the blocks again; then invite several children to work together to complete the same task, applauding their efforts as well. After jotting down their time, help youngsters make a comparison to decide which method is faster. Then lead a discussion about the importance of teamwork.

Teamwork Is for Everyone!

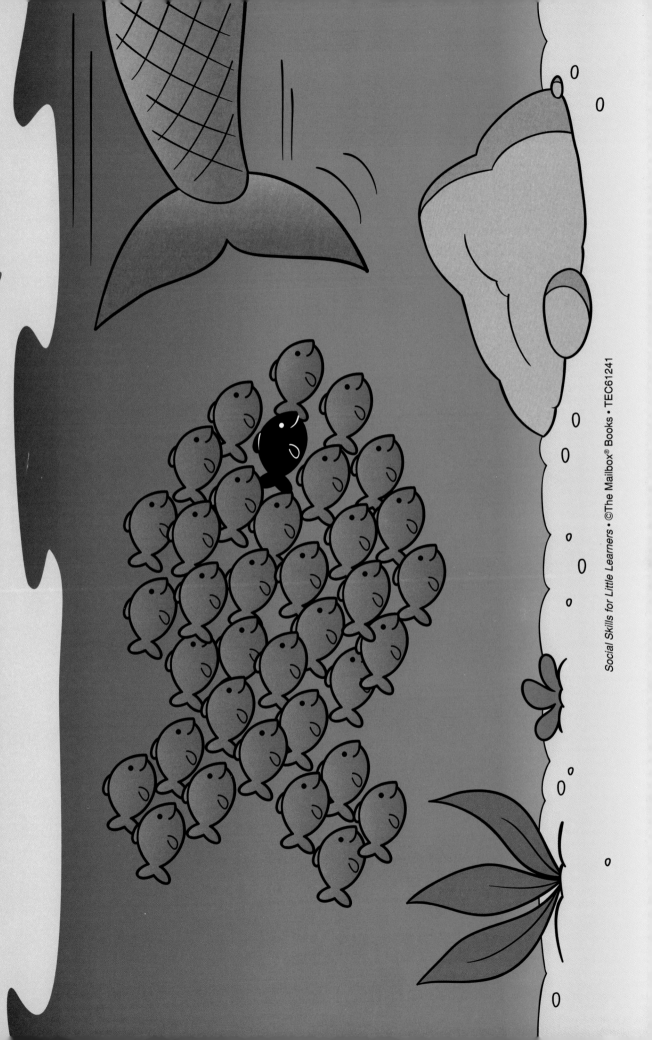

Teamwork Is for Everyone!

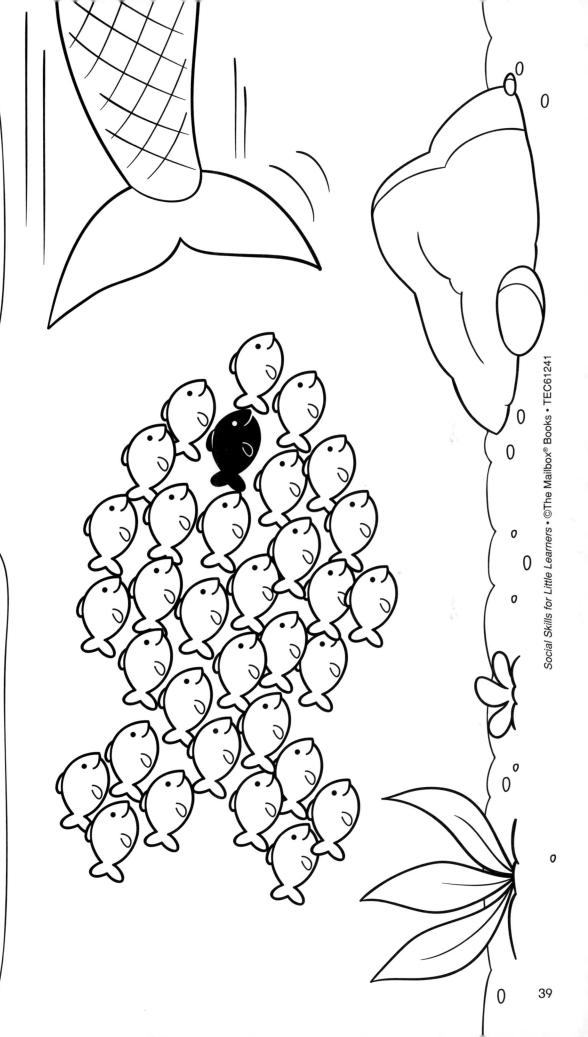

Fish Patterns

Use with "Go Away, Tuna!" on page 35 and "Under the Sea" on page 36.

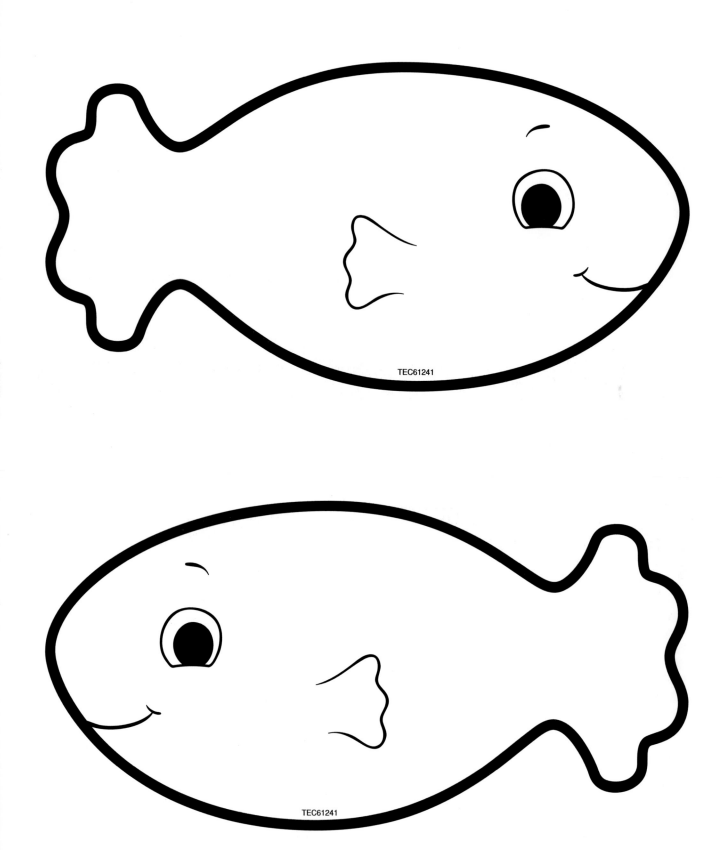

TEC61241

TEC61241

Social Skills for Little Learners • ©The Mailbox® Books • TEC61241

Think Before You Act!

Read aloud a favorite version of *Chicken Little* (or *Henny Penny*) to help students learn that they should gather the facts before they react. Then engage youngsters in this selection of activities that will guide them in learning self-control.

Plop!

After reading aloud the story, ask youngsters to name things Chicken Little could have done to show self-control when the acorn hit his head, such as finding out what hit him and taking a deep breath to calm down. Help students generate several strategies to use when upset and record them on an oversize acorn cutout. Then invite youngsters, in turn, to pretend to be Chicken Little. As each child walks along, drop a large brown pom-pom (acorn) on her head and have her demonstrate one of the strategies listed.

Stop and Think!

Chicken Little uses self-control in this engaging rhyme! Have each child make a stick puppet that shows the main character in the version of the story read to your students (see page 46 for patterns). Read aloud the poem shown, encouraging youngsters to chant the last line of each stanza with you while holding their puppets in the air.

Chicken Little felt something fall from the sky.
It hit his head! He wanted to cry!
Stop and think, Chicken Little!

Rather than guessing what hit his head,
He stopped to look around instead.
Stop and think, Chicken Little!

He looked on the ground, and what he saw
Was an acorn nearby! The sky didn't fall!
Stop and think, Chicken Little!

Chicken Little moved from under the tree
So he wouldn't get hit again, you see.
Stop and think, Chicken Little!

In Control

This idea encourages the whole class to practice self-control! Make a simple display similar to the one shown (see page 46 for character patterns). Then discuss with youngsters scenarios that sometimes cause self-control issues, such as sharing and turn taking. Ask students to name ways to show self-control in each situation. Throughout the week when self-control is shown, record student behavior on separate acorn cutouts. Then invite each child to attach his acorn to the display.

One, Two, Think It Through!

The story might have turned out differently if Chicken Little had known this nifty chant! Teach your little ones the chant shown to help them keep their cool and think things through!

One, two, think it through.
Three, four, think some more.
Five, six, the clock ticks.
Seven, eight, still I wait.
Nine, ten, now I'm ready again!

Cool-Down Station

With this idea, preschoolers have the space they need to help regain their self-control! Use the patterns on pages 47 and 48 to make a train display at students' eye level. Attach to the boxcars photographs of youngsters playing nicely and title the display "Cool-Down Station." Place pillows and a basket of stress balls in the area. Have a child visit the area when she is having difficulty maintaining self-control. After she is calm, point out one of the photos of children showing self-control; then discuss making choices like those displayed.

Think Before You Act!

Think Before You Act!

Chick and Hen Patterns

Use with "Stop and Think!" on page 41 and "In Control" on page 42.

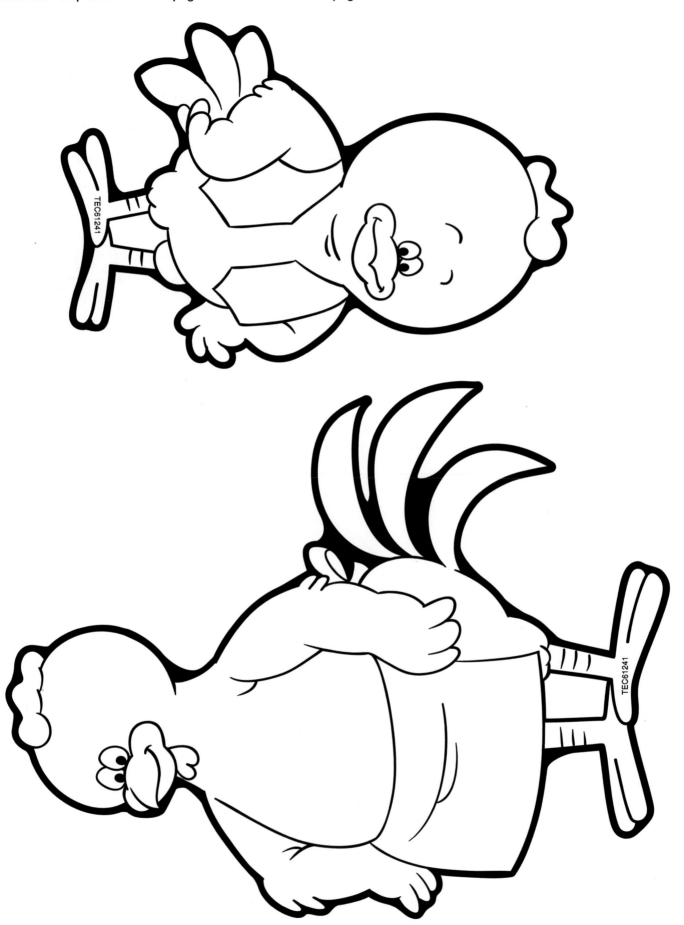

TEC61241

Boxcar Pattern

Use with "Cool-Down Station" on page 42.

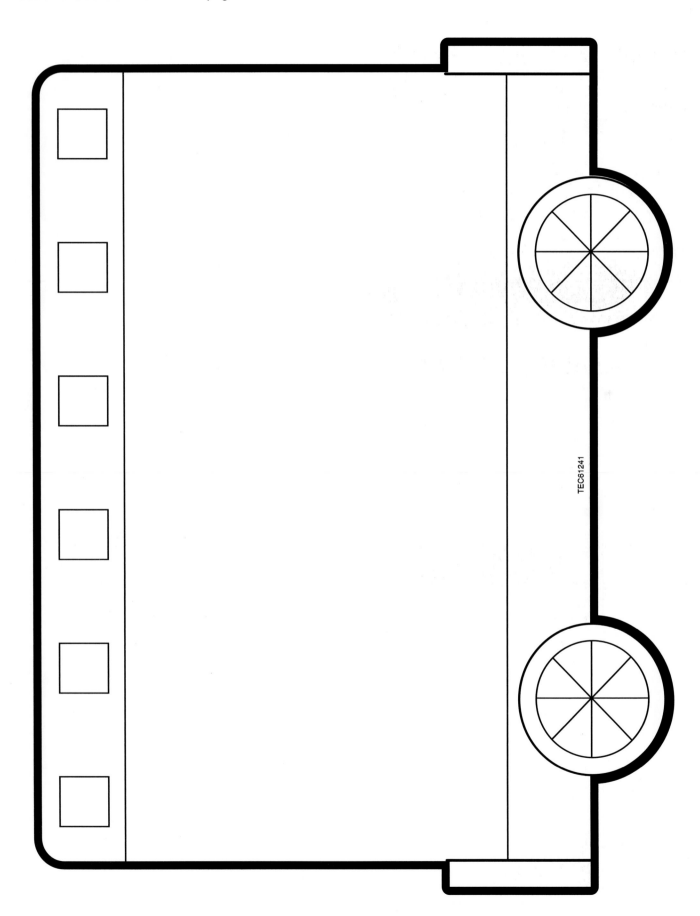

TEC61241

Social Skills for Little Learners • ©The Mailbox® Books • TEC61241

Let's Work Together!

Help your little ones understand the importance of cooperation by reading aloud your favorite version of *The Little Red Hen*. Then invite youngsters to engage in these fun-filled cooperative activities! Rest assured, no one will say, "Not I!"

Freshly Baked Bread!

After hearing what happens to the lazy animals in the story, youngsters are sure to say, "I will!" when asked, "Who will help bake some bread?" To prepare for this exercise in cooperation, obtain quick bread mix. Then help youngsters work together to prepare the mix. Bake the mix according to the package directions. Then serve each of your little bakers a slice of freshly baked bread along with a side order of compliments for their cooperative effort!

Story Center

Students show off their cooperation skills when they work together to sequence the hen's many tasks. Color and cut out a copy of each pattern from pages 54 and 55. Then place the cutouts at a center along with a copy of *The Little Red Hen*. Encourage small groups of youngsters to visit the center and order the cutouts to show the sequence from seeds of grain to a fabulous loaf of bread.

Growing Feathers

In advance, color and cut out an enlarged copy of the hen pattern from page 56. Then attach it to your wall. Make a supply of red feather cutouts. Ask youngsters, "What do you think our classroom would be like if we behaved like the Little Red Hen's friends?" After giving students time to respond, discuss the importance of cooperation and the benefits of working together. Each time you observe children cooperating, record your observation on a feather and attach it to the hen. Read aloud each feather and praise youngsters for their cooperative behavior!

Tasty Topping!

Divide your class into small groups. Then give each group a small plastic jar half-filled with heavy whipping cream. Have a child in each group shake the jar vigorously as you lead the remaining youngsters in singing the song shown. When the song ends, have her pass the jar to her neighbor. Continue in the same way until each group's whipping cream has turned into butter (about ten minutes). Strain any liquid from the jar. Then invite each student to spread some of the delicious homemade butter on a slice of her freshly baked bread (see page 49). Now that's cooperation with some tasty results!

(sung to the tune of "Skip to My Lou")

Shake, shake, shake the jar.
Shake, shake, shake it hard.
Shake, shake, shake the jar.
Soon we will have butter!

Seeds of Cooperation

Guide youngsters through this planting activity to help demonstrate the importance of cooperation! Gather five students and give each child one of the items shown. Then ask each youngster if he has everything he needs to plant the seeds. Lead students to conclude that they each have only one of the items needed for planting, but as a group, they have all the necessary items. Encourage the youngsters to work together to plant the seeds in the pot.

POTTING SOIL

Seeds

Let's Work Together!

Let's Work Together!

53

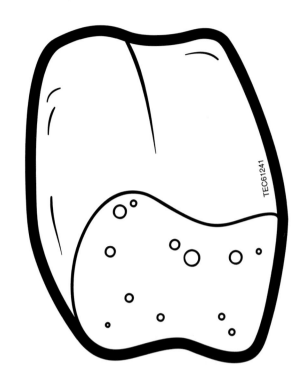

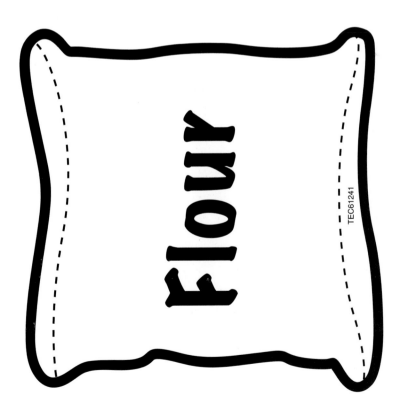

Hen Pattern
Use with "Growing Feathers" on page 50.

TEC61241

Being Brave

Read aloud a favorite version of *The Three Little Pigs* to get youngsters ready for a selection of ideas on the theme of courage. Little ones are sure to agree that the brave little pigs hold their own against the huffing and puffing wolf!

Speak Up!

"Not by the hair of my chinny chin chin!" each courageous pig said to the big bad wolf. Have students name other ways the pigs could speak up when the wolf knocks on their doors. For example, they might say, "Go away" or "I'm calling 9-1-1!" List student responses on your board. Then invite volunteers to hold character stick puppets (see page 62) and role-play the wolf knocking on the pig's door. Encourage the child with the pig puppet to respond with one of the listed responses.

Little pig, little pig, let me come in.

I'm calling 9-1-1!

Brave Little Builders

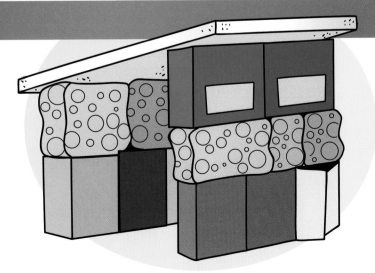

It takes a lot of courage for each pig to set out on his own and build a house. With this idea, your youngsters can be brave builders as well! In advance, stock your block center with a variety of unique building materials, such as sponges or empty food boxes. Then discuss how the pigs were courageous and invite students to share their own courageous experiences. When a youngster goes to the block center, he pretends to be one of the pigs and uses the items to build a unique house.

The Pigs' Houses

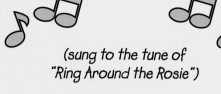

(sung to the tune of
"Ring Around the Rosie")

Little piggies playing.
The big bad wolf comes preying.
Huff and puff and
The house falls down!

To prepare for this game, use masking tape to make a rectangle on your floor to represent a pig's house. Have students hold hands and walk in a circle as they sing the song shown. At the end of the song, instruct students to move quickly and stand in the house so they are safe from the big bad wolf. Once all your little ones are in the house, invite them to discuss how the first two pigs might have felt as they were running to a new house, leading them to conclude that even though the pigs were probably scared, they needed to act courageously.

Snacktime Courage

Gather several uncommon fruits. For each student, prepare a plate with a small sample of each fruit. Have students look at their plates and invite them to share reasons they would or would not like to try these fruits. Tell students that it takes courage to try new foods and encourage them to taste each fruit. Then have each child complete a copy of page 63 to take home to show her family.

Badge of Courage

Invite little ones to discuss ways they are courageous, such as saying goodbye to their parents each morning or staying calm during a thunderstorm. Then give each child a badge cutout (see page 64). Have her draw on the badge a picture that illustrates a time she was courageous. Then help her write her name and complete the sentence.

Be Brave

Be Brave

TEC61241

TEC61241

Social Skills for Little Learners • ©The Mailbox® Books • TEC61241

Name _____

I tried new fruits today.
This was my plate.

Note to the teacher: Use with "Snacktime Courage" on page 58.

Badge Pattern

Use with "Badge of Courage" on page 58.

was courageous by

TEC61241

Sharing Shows Kindness

Show your little ones how a generous family shares its cookies with lots of unexpected guests in a read-aloud of *The Doorbell Rang* by Pat Hutchins. Then invite youngsters to follow suit with this collection of fun ideas about sharing!

Enough for Everyone!

Highlight your youngsters' sharing skills with this fun reenactment of the story! Provide eight craft foam cookies and eight paper plates. Give each of two students a plate; then have them work together to divide the cookies evenly between them. Next, say, "No one makes cookies like Grandma!" Then have the remaining students chant, "Ding-dong!" and have two more children come to share the cookies. Repeat the process one more time, this time inviting four more children to share.

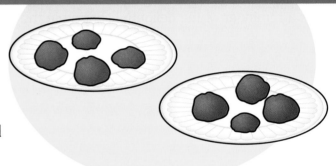

One Cookie to Share

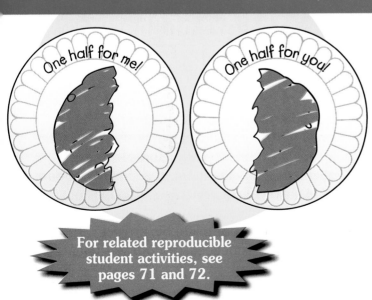

One half for me!

One half for you!

Victoria and Sam happily share a batch of cookies freshly baked by Grandma! But what if they had only one cookie to share? After eliciting ideas on what the pair could do, invite each child to make a cookie for two! To begin, have each child color and cut out a cookie pattern from a copy of page 70. Next, have her tear the cookie in half and then glue one half to a paper plate labeled "One half for me!" and the remaining half to a plate labeled "One half for you!" Then have each child give her second plate to a class-mate. If desired, mount the plates on a board with a large cookie jar cutout and title the display "Cookies for Two."

For related reproducible student activities, see pages 71 and 72.

Knock, Knock!

Arrange for a coworker to bring a tray of cookies to your classroom and knock on the door. After your visitor arrives with the yummy surprise, divide your class into several small groups. Give each group a plate containing enough cookies for each child within the group to have two. Then have students in each group work together to distribute the cookies evenly among themselves. Top off the cooperative sharing with cold milk for everyone!

Yummy Cookies!

Lead youngsters in singing this cute song as a reminder of the delightful sharing in the story.

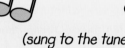

(sung to the tune of
"Did You Ever See a Lassie?")

Oh, we have some yummy cookies,
So munchy and crunchy.
Yes, we have some yummy cookies.
Oh, what should we do?
We'll share them with you
And you and you.
Yes, sharing is the right thing,
The right thing to do!

The Art of Sharing

This activity challenges students to think of creative ways to share! Place at your art center a supply of paper, two pairs of scissors, two glue sticks, and one magazine. Have a small group of students join you at the center. Invite each child to cut pictures from the magazine and glue them to a sheet of paper to make a collage. Encourage youngsters to brainstorm ways to share the materials so each child can complete his project. Provide suggestions as needed and praise students' efforts to share!

Sharing Shows Kindness

Sharing Shows Kindness

Cookie Patterns

Use with "One Cookie to Share" on page 65.

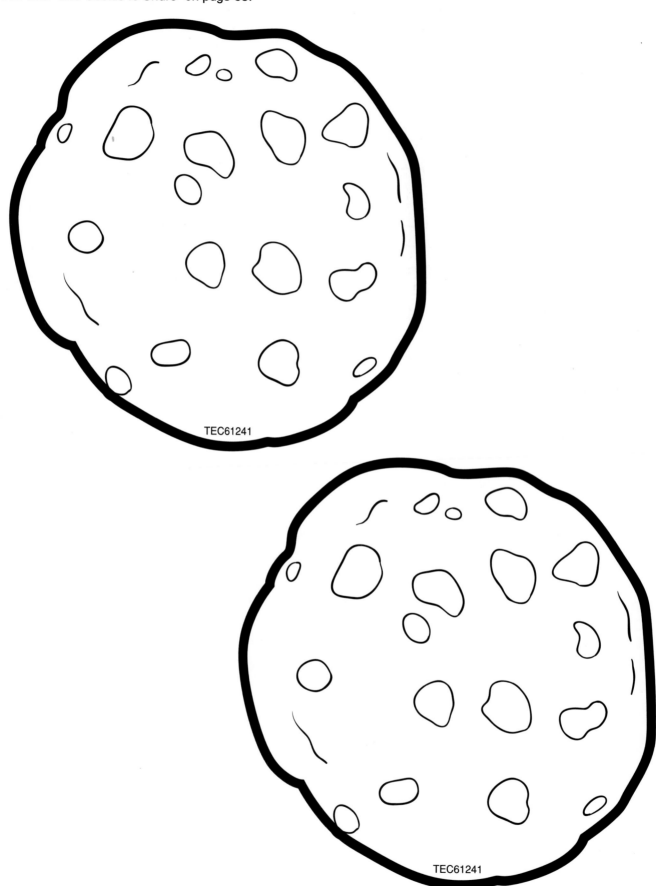

TEC61241

TEC61241

I can share my snack.

I can share toys.

I can share a hug!

I Can Share!

Name _____

Social Skills for Little Learners • ©The Mailbox® Books • TEC61241

Fold-and-Go Booklet: To make a booklet, cut on the bold line. Fold along the thin horizontal line (keeping the programming to the outside) and then fold along the thin vertical line (keeping the cover to the outside). Have each child color his booklet pages.

71

Sharing Feels Great!

If I had _____ ,

I would share it with

by _____

Class book page: Have each child write or dictate a response to the prompt. Then have her illustrate and personalize her work. Publish the pages in a class book titled "Sharing Shows Caring."

Let's All Get Along!

Set the stage for these fun-filled activities by reading aloud a favorite version of *The Three Billy Goats Gruff.* Your preschoolers surely will agree that the mean-spirited troll needs coaching to learn to get along with others!

Very Grumpy!

What's with that troll's grumpy voice? Use your most grumpy voice to ask the question, "Who is crossing my bridge?" and then repeat the question with a calm voice. Give students a moment to think about how each version of the question made them feel. Next, have students repeat the question using their most grumpy voices and again using calm voices. Talk more about how the tone of a person's voice affects how the listener feels about what is being said. For added fun and effect, repeat the activity using additional phrases spoken by the troll and phrases familiar to students too.

What If?

What if the troll hadn't been so mean and grumpy? Could the goats and the troll have become friends? Engage students in role-playing alternative story lines that show a friendlier and more thoughtful troll. To add to the fun, give a pair of rhythm sticks to each student who is not playing a role. Prompt these youngsters to tap the sticks together when appropriate to imitate the sound of each billy goat crossing the bridge. Make sure the loudness of the tapping reflects the size of each goat!

Storytelling Puppets

Use the patterns on pages 78 and 79 to put any number of billy goat and troll puppets at your block center. To make a puppet, color and cut out a pattern; fold it along the thin line, keeping the artwork to the outside. Next, slide one end of a jumbo craft stick between the inside surfaces and glue them together. Show students both the grumpy side and the kind side of the troll puppet before you place all the puppets at the center. Encourage students to use the blocks and the puppets to tell stories that show the benefits of getting along with others!

Big and Green
(sung to the tune of "I'm a Little Teapot")

I'm an ugly troll. I'm big and green.
I used to shout and be very mean.
I yelled and grumbled—that was my way.
No one asked me out to play.

I'm an ugly troll. I'm big and green.
But I have changed—I'm no longer mean!
I am nice and have kind things to say.
I can share. Please, come and play!

A New Attitude

With all the tips your little ones are giving the troll, he's surely ready to turn over a new leaf! Celebrate a wiser and kinder troll with this catchy tune that's fun to sing *and* act out!

Class Collage

Turn a sticky situation into an occasion for little ones to show how well they get along! First, have little ones work together to tear colorful paper scraps into smaller pieces. Next, have the students press the torn paper pieces onto the sticky side of a large piece of clear Con-Tact covering until the entire surface is covered. As students are working, recognize the positive behaviors you see. Then trim the artwork into a large heart and display the cutout as a positive reminder of the benefits of getting along with each other.

For a related reproducible student activity, go to page 80.

Let's All Get Along!

Let's All Get Along!

Goat Patterns

Use with "Storytelling Puppets" on page 74.

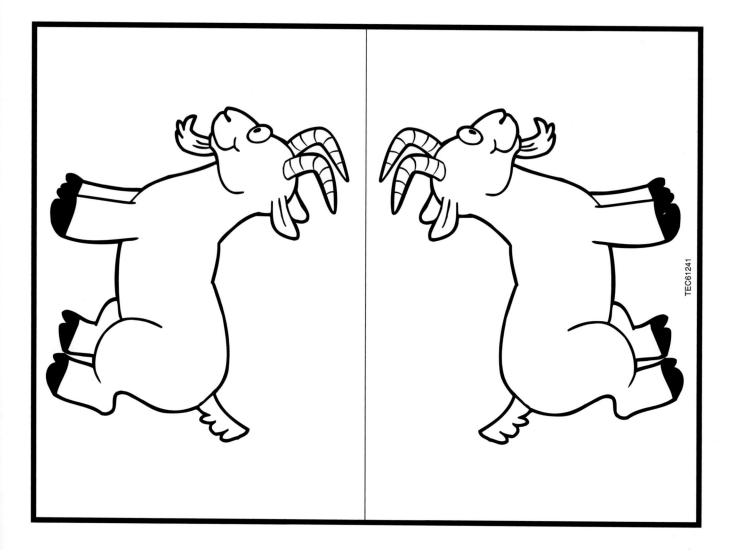

TEC61241

TEC61241

Name _____

80

Best Behavior

Social Skills for Little Learners • ©The Mailbox® Books • TEC61241

Note to the teacher: Briefly describe what is happening in each illustration. Help the student decide whether the behavior demonstrates getting along with others. If the behavior does, he colors the picture. If it does not, he crosses out the picture.